The Neuroscience of Gratitude: How Cultivating Appreciation Rewires Your Brain

Casley Jude

Table of Contents

Casley Jude 1

Contents .... **Error! Bookmark not defined.**

Introduction 4

    A personal story or anecdote illustrating the transformative nature of gratitude 5

    The concept of neuroplasticity and how it relates to the brain's ability to change and adapt ... 7

Chapter 1: Understanding Gratitude 9

    Evolutionary Origins of Gratitude and Its Significance in Human Psychology 11

    Benefits of practicing gratitude, including improved well-being, mental health, and relationships 13

Chapter 2: The Brain and Its Marvels 15

    Basic overview of the brain's structure and function 17

    Role of neurotransmitters, such as dopamine and serotonin, in regulating emotions and mood 19

    The concept of neural pathways and their importance in shaping behavior and thought patterns 20

Chapter 3: Unraveling Neuroplasticity 23

    Mechanisms of neuroplasticity, including synaptic pruning, neurogenesis, and myelination ..27

    Examples of neuroplasticity in action and how it relates to gratitude 29

Chapter 4: Gratitude and the Brain 31

    Scientific studies and research on the neural correlates of gratitude 33

    Brain regions associated with gratitude, such as the prefrontal cortex, amygdala, and insula 35

    Neurochemical changes observed during gratitude practices and their impact on well-being 37

Chapter 5: Rewiring the Brain with Gratitude Practices 39

    Practical techniques for cultivating gratitude, such as gratitude journaling, meditation, and acts of kindness 41

    How consistent gratitude practices can reshape neural pathways and strengthen positive emotions 44

    Real-life examples and success stories to inspire readers to incorporate gratitude into their daily lives 46

Chapter 6: Integrating Gratitude into Relationships 48

    The role of gratitude in fostering healthy relationships and connections 50

    Tips on expressing gratitude to loved ones and creating a gratitude culture within families, friendships, and workplaces 53

    The reciprocal nature of gratitude and its potential to enhance social bonds 55

Chapter 7: Gratitude as a Tool for Resilience and Mental Health 58

    How gratitude practices can boost resilience and help manage stress, anxiety, and depression 60

    The link between gratitude and self-esteem, self-worth, and overall mental well-being 62

    Evidence-based strategies for incorporating gratitude into therapy and personal growth 64

Conclusion 67

Introduction

Welcome, dear readers, to a journey of discovery into the incredible realm of gratitude and its profound impact on the human brain. In a world often filled with chaos and uncertainty, it is easy to overlook the simple yet transformative practice of expressing appreciation. But as we delve into the fascinating world of neuroscience, we will uncover the immense power of gratitude and how it has the potential to reshape our very minds.

In this eBook, we will embark on a captivating exploration of the neuroscience of gratitude. We will venture beyond the surface and delve into the intricate workings of the brain, where the seeds of gratitude take root and bloom into profound change. Prepare to be amazed as we unravel the mysteries of neuroplasticity and witness how gratitude, when nurtured, can rewire the intricate pathways of our minds.

Gratitude is more than a mere concept; it is a potent force that can revolutionize our lives. Countless individuals have experienced its transformative effects, and scientific research has provided us with a deeper understanding of how gratitude impacts our mental and emotional well-being. From enhancing our overall happiness to boosting our resilience in the face of challenges, gratitude has the potential to reshape our brains and open new avenues for growth and fulfillment.

As we embark on this enlightening journey together, let us embrace the power of gratitude, transcending cultural boundaries and personal experiences. It is my hope that by the end of this eBook, you will not only be armed with knowledge but also inspired to incorporate gratitude into your daily life.

So, dear readers, fasten your seatbelts and get ready to witness the captivating dance between gratitude and the brain. Let us unveil the extraordinary power that lies within us to transform our lives, one grateful thought at a time.

A personal story or anecdote illustrating the transformative nature of gratitude

I vividly remember a moment in my life when gratitude revealed its extraordinary ability to shift my perspective and bring about profound change. Several years ago, I found myself navigating through a particularly challenging period. I was overwhelmed by stress, consumed by negativity, and trapped in a cycle of discontent. It seemed as though every aspect of my life was shrouded in gloom, and I struggled to find a way out.

In the midst of this darkness, a close friend suggested I try practicing gratitude as a means of finding solace and clarity. Sceptical yet desperate for a glimmer of hope, I decided to give it a try. I committed to keeping a gratitude journal, where I would write down three things I was grateful for each day.

In the beginning, it felt like a mere ritual, an exercise in wishful thinking. But as I persisted, something remarkable began to unfold within me. The simple act of acknowledging and appreciating the blessings in my life started to shift my focus from what was lacking to what I already had. I began to notice the small joys that had previously gone unnoticed—

the warmth of sunlight on my face, the laughter shared with loved ones, and the comforting aroma of freshly brewed coffee.

With each passing day, my gratitude journal became a sacred space where I poured my heart out, acknowledging even the tiniest moments of beauty and grace. Slowly but surely, my perspective began to shift, and a newfound sense of peace and contentment seeped into my being. The weight of negativity gradually lifted, replaced by a profound sense of appreciation and wonder.

As my practice of gratitude deepened, I noticed tangible changes in my daily life. I became more resilient in the face of challenges, finding hidden opportunities for growth and learning. Relationships blossomed as I expressed heartfelt gratitude to those around me, fostering deeper connections and a sense of belonging. Even my overall well-being improved, as the relentless grip of stress loosened its hold on me.

This personal journey taught me that gratitude is not just a fleeting emotion; it is a transformative state of being. It has the power to reframe our experiences, rewiring our brains to perceive the world through a lens of abundance and possibility. My own story is just one testament to the remarkable potential that lies within each of us to cultivate gratitude and nurture its profound impact on our lives.

As we embark on this exploration of gratitude's effects on the brain, I invite you to reflect on your own experiences. Perhaps you too have encountered moments of gratitude that have shifted your perspective or brought about positive change. Together, let us uncover the science behind these transformative experiences and unlock the extraordinary potential of gratitude within ourselves and the world around us.

The concept of neuroplasticity and how it relates to the brain's ability to change and adapt

To understand the profound impact of gratitude on the brain, we must first explore the fascinating concept of neuroplasticity. Contrary to the long-held belief that the brain remains fixed and unchanging throughout adulthood, research has revealed that our brains possess an extraordinary capacity to adapt, grow, and rewire themselves throughout our lives.

Neuroplasticity refers to the brain's ability to form new neural connections, reorganize existing ones, and even generate new neurons. It is a dynamic process that occurs in response to our experiences, thoughts, and behaviors. This means that our brains are not static entities but rather malleable and constantly evolving structures.

Think of the brain as a complex network of pathways, where information travels through electrical and chemical signals. When we engage in specific thoughts or behaviors repeatedly, these neural pathways become strengthened, forming well-worn tracks that shape our perceptions, emotions, and actions. Conversely, neglected pathways weaken and fade away.

Neuroplasticity encompasses several mechanisms that facilitate these changes. One such mechanism is synaptic plasticity, which involves the strengthening or weakening of connections between neurons called synapses. Through a process called long-term potentiation, repeated activation of a particular neural pathway enhances the efficiency of signal transmission, making that pathway more accessible and influential in our thoughts and behaviors.

Additionally, neuroplasticity involves neurogenesis, the birth of new neurons, primarily in the hippocampus—a region of the brain associated with learning and memory. It was once believed that the adult brain could not generate new neurons, but we now know that neurogenesis can occur throughout life, albeit to a lesser extent than during early development. This discovery further emphasizes the brain's remarkable ability to adapt and change.

So, how does neuroplasticity relate to gratitude? When we practice gratitude consistently, we activate specific neural pathways associated with positive emotions, empathy, and well-being. By intentionally focusing on the things we are grateful for, we strengthen these pathways, making gratitude a more natural and automatic response. Over time, this rewiring shapes our brain to perceive the world through a lens of gratitude, enabling us to find joy in the smallest of moments and navigate life's challenges with resilience.

Understanding neuroplasticity allows us to appreciate the immense power we hold to shape our brains and, consequently, our experiences. By actively cultivating gratitude, we have the ability to rewire our neural circuitry, leading to lasting positive changes in our thoughts, emotions, and overall well-being. The science of neuroplasticity offers us hope and empowers us to take an active role in nurturing gratitude within ourselves and transforming our lives for the better.

Chapter 1: Understanding Gratitude

In this chapter, we will delve into the essence of gratitude and explore its profound impact on our lives. We will embark on a journey to understand the various facets of gratitude, its evolutionary origins, and the multitude of benefits it offers. By gaining a deeper comprehension of gratitude, we lay the foundation for exploring its transformative effects on the brain.

Defining Gratitude: Gratitude is a multifaceted concept that encompasses more than a simple "thank you." At its core, gratitude is a deep appreciation and recognition of the positive aspects of our lives, including the people, experiences, and circumstances that bring us joy and fulfillment. It goes beyond mere politeness and taps into a wellspring of positive emotions that can enhance our well-being.

Evolutionary Origins of Gratitude: Gratitude is not merely a social construct; it has deep roots in human evolution. Our ancestors relied on cooperative behavior and social bonds for survival. Gratitude served as a mechanism to strengthen these social connections and promote reciprocal relationships, fostering cooperation, and group cohesion. By understanding gratitude's evolutionary origins, we gain insight into its fundamental importance in human psychology.

The Benefits of Practicing Gratitude: The practice of gratitude extends far beyond a fleeting feeling of appreciation. Numerous scientific studies have highlighted the wide-ranging benefits that gratitude offers. When we cultivate gratitude in our lives, we can experience improvements in our overall well-being, mental health, and relationships. Gratitude has been linked to increased happiness, reduced stress and anxiety, improved sleep quality, enhanced self-esteem, and stronger social connections.

Gratitude as a Mindset: Gratitude is not limited to isolated moments of thankfulness. It can become a way of life—a mindset that colors our perception of the world. By adopting a gratitude mindset, we shift our focus from what is lacking to what we already have. This shift in perspective allows us to cultivate contentment, resilience, and a deeper sense of fulfillment. We will explore the transformative power of gratitude as a mindset and its impact on our daily lives.

The Practice of Gratitude: Gratitude is not a passive state; it is an active practice that requires intention and effort. We will explore various gratitude practices and techniques that can help us cultivate appreciation in our lives. From keeping a gratitude journal to engaging in gratitude meditation and performing acts of kindness, these practices provide us with practical tools to nurture gratitude and reap its countless benefits.

The Neuroscience of Gratitude: As we embark on this journey of understanding gratitude, we will also explore the neuroscience behind its effects. Emerging research has shed light on the neural correlates of gratitude, uncovering specific brain regions and neurochemicals that are involved. We will delve into the fascinating scientific findings that demonstrate how gratitude can shape the brain and its functioning.

By delving into the depths of understanding gratitude, we lay the groundwork for harnessing its transformative power. As we navigate this chapter, we invite you to reflect on your own experiences with gratitude and begin to recognize the immense potential it holds for reshaping our lives. Together, let us embark on this exploration of gratitude and its profound effects on our well-being and the intricate workings of the brain.

Evolutionary Origins of Gratitude and Its Significance in Human Psychology

Gratitude, with its roots deep in human evolution, holds significant meaning in our psychology and social interactions. To fully comprehend the power of gratitude, it is essential to explore its evolutionary origins and understand why it has become such an integral part of the human experience.

As social creatures, our early ancestors relied on cooperation and group cohesion for survival. In the face of challenging environments and the need to navigate threats and scarce resources, forming and maintaining social bonds became crucial. Gratitude played a vital role in facilitating these connections.

The evolutionary roots of gratitude can be traced back to our ancestral environment, where expressions of appreciation and reciprocation were vital for promoting cooperation and maintaining harmonious relationships within social groups. By acknowledging and reciprocating the help, protection, and support received from others, our ancestors solidified their social bonds and fostered a sense of collective well-being.

Gratitude, then, served as a mechanism to reinforce prosocial behavior. Individuals who expressed gratitude were more likely to receive continued support from their peers, ensuring their survival and success within the group. In this way, gratitude became intertwined with our evolutionary history, shaping our social interactions and psychological well-being.

In modern times, although our survival no longer depends solely on cooperation within a small social group, the significance of gratitude remains deeply ingrained in our psychology. Gratitude continues to foster a sense of social connection and reciprocity, which positively impacts our relationships and overall well-being.

Expressing gratitude allows us to acknowledge and value the contributions of others, strengthening social bonds and fostering a sense of belonging. When we express gratitude, it not only benefits the recipient but also enhances our own psychological state. It promotes a positive emotional climate, cultivates empathy and compassion, and encourages acts of kindness and cooperation.

Furthermore, gratitude shifts our focus from a mindset of scarcity to one of abundance. By recognizing and appreciating what we already have, we cultivate contentment and reduce the tendency to constantly strive for more. This shift in perspective enhances our overall satisfaction with life and promotes psychological resilience, enabling us to navigate challenges with a sense of optimism and gratitude.

Understanding the evolutionary origins of gratitude offers profound insights into its significance in human psychology. By acknowledging and nurturing gratitude in our lives, we tap into a powerful force that strengthens our social connections, enhances our well-being, and shapes our perceptions of the world. In the following chapters, we will delve deeper into the neuroscience of gratitude, unraveling the intricate workings of the brain and uncovering how gratitude rewires our neural circuitry, bringing about lasting positive change.

Benefits of practicing gratitude, including improved well-being, mental health, and relationships

The practice of gratitude offers a multitude of benefits that extend far beyond mere appreciation. When we actively cultivate gratitude in our lives, we unlock a range of positive outcomes that positively impact our well-being, mental health, and relationships. Let us explore some of the remarkable benefits that arise from practicing gratitude.

Increased Happiness: Gratitude has a profound effect on our overall happiness and life satisfaction. When we regularly express gratitude for the blessings in our lives, we shift our focus towards the positive aspects, fostering a greater sense of joy and contentment. Grateful individuals are more likely to experience higher levels of happiness and a greater sense of fulfillment.

Reduced Stress and Anxiety: Gratitude serves as a powerful antidote to stress and anxiety. By focusing on the things we are grateful for, we redirect our attention away from worry and rumination. Gratitude enhances oan opportunity cope with stress, lowers cortisol levels (the stress hormone), and promotes a sense of calm and emotional well-being.

Improved Mental Health: Gratitude plays a crucial role in promoting positive mental health. Studies have shown that practicing gratitude is associated with lower levels of depression, decreased symptoms of anxiety, and greater psychological resilience. Grateful individuals tend to have a more optimistic outlook and are better equipped to handle life's challenges.

Enhanced Relationships: Gratitude has a transformative effect on our relationships, both romantic and platonic. Expressing gratitude towards our loved ones strengthens the bond between us, fosters feelings of closeness and trust, and cultivates a sense of appreciation and reciprocity. Gratitude acts as a relational lubricant, promoting healthier and more satisfying connections with others.

Improved Physical Health: The benefits of gratitude extend beyond mental well-being and impact our physical health as well. Grateful individuals have been found to experience better sleep quality, lower blood pressure, and a stronger immune system. By reducing stress and promoting positive emotions, gratitude contributes to our overall physical well-being.

Increased Resilience: Gratitude equips us with the tools to navigate life's challenges with resilience and grace. When we actively practice gratitude, we develop a positive mindset that helps us reframe adversity as opportunities for growth. Grateful individuals are better able to bounce back from setbacks, maintain a positive outlook, and find meaning in difficult experiences.

By incorporating gratitude into our daily lives, we tap into a wellspring of benefits that positively impact our well-being, mental health, and relationships. These benefits extend to various domains of life, allowing us to experience greater happiness, reduced stress, improved mental health, and stronger connections with others. In the following chapters, we will further explore the practical techniques and exercises that can help us harness the power of gratitude and unlock its transformative effects.

Chapter 2: The Brain and Its Marvels

In this chapter, we will embark on a captivating exploration of the brain and its remarkable capabilities. By understanding the intricate workings of this complex organ, we can unravel the mysteries behind how gratitude influences and shapes our neural landscape. Join us on this journey as we delve into the fascinating world of the brain and its marvels.

The Brain: The Seat of Our Experiences The brain is an awe-inspiring organ that serves as the command center of our bodies and the seat of our experiences. It is composed of billions of neurons, nerve cells that communicate with each other through intricate networks. These networks form the foundation of our thoughts, emotions, memories, and behaviors. By unraveling the inner workings of the brain, we gain insight into the biological underpinnings of gratitude and its effects on our mental and emotional well-being.

Neurons and Neural Pathways Neurons are the fundamental building blocks of the brain. These specialized cells receive and transmit electrical and chemical signals, allowing information to flow throughout the brain. Neural pathways are the routes that information takes as it travels between different regions of the brain. These pathways are responsible for processing sensory input, generating thoughts and emotions, and controlling our actions. Understanding the formation and plasticity of these pathways is key to comprehending how gratitude can shape the brain.

Neurotransmitters and Neurochemicals Neurotransmitters and neurochemicals play a pivotal role in facilitating communication between neurons. These chemical messengers transmit signals across synapses, the tiny gaps between neurons. Neurotransmitters such as dopamine, serotonin, and oxytocin are closely linked to our emotions, mood, and social bonding. We will explore how gratitude influences the release and activity of these neurochemicals, contributing to positive emotional states and enhanced social connections.

Neuroplasticity: The Brain's Adaptive Power Neuroplasticity, the brain's remarkable ability to change and adapt, is a central theme in understanding how gratitude impacts the brain. We will delve deeper into the mechanisms of neuroplasticity, including synaptic plasticity and neurogenesis. These processes allow the brain to rewire itself, forming new connections and strengthening existing ones. By practicing gratitude, we harness the power of neuroplasticity to shape our neural networks and enhance our well-being.

The Default Mode Network The Default Mode Network (DMN) is a network of brain regions that is active during restful states and self-referential thinking. It plays a crucial role in our sense of self, introspection, and mind-wandering. Emerging research suggests that gratitude can influence the activity and connectivity within the DMN, leading to a greater sense of self-awareness, improved emotional regulation, and reduced rumination.

The Social Brain: Empathy and Compassion The brain is wired for social connection, and gratitude plays a significant role in our social interactions. We will explore the brain regions involved in empathy and compassion, such as the anterior cingulate cortex and the insula. By understanding how gratitude activates these regions, we can comprehend the neural mechanisms underlying our capacity for empathy and the cultivation of compassion toward others.

As we delve into the marvels of the brain, we gain insight into the intricate dance between gratitude and neural processes. By understanding the brain's adaptability, neurotransmitters, neuroplasticity, and social networks, we unlock the potential to harness gratitude's transformative power. Join us as we uncover the scientific discoveries that illuminate the fascinating interplay between gratitude and the brain, paving the way for a deeper understanding of how gratitude changes our minds and lives.

Basic overview of the brain's structure and function

The brain, a complex and intricately organized organ, is responsible for coordinating and controlling all our thoughts, emotions, sensations, and actions. It consists of several interconnected regions, each with unique functions and contributions to our overall cognitive and physiological processes. Here is a basic overview of the brain's structure and function:

> **Cerebrum:** The cerebrum is the largest and most prominent part of the brain, divided into two cerebral hemispheres: the left hemisphere and the right hemisphere. Each hemisphere is further divided into four lobes: the frontal lobe, parietal lobe, temporal lobe, and occipital lobe. The cerebrum is associated with higher-level cognitive functions such as perception, consciousness, memory, language, and decision-making.

> **Cerebellum:** Located at the back of the brain, below the cerebrum, the cerebellum is responsible for coordinating movement, balance, and posture. It helps regulate muscle tone and fine-tunes motor skills, allowing for smooth and coordinated movements.

Brainstem: The brainstem is the region connecting the spinal cord to the rest of the brain. It consists of three parts: the medulla oblongata, the pons, and the midbrain. The brainstem controls essential functions necessary for survival, such as breathing, heart rate, digestion, and sleep-wake cycles.

Limbic System: The limbic system, situated deep within the brain, plays a crucial role in emotions, memory, and motivation. It includes structures like the amygdala, hippocampus, thalamus, and hypothalamus. The limbic system helps regulate our emotional responses, facilitates memory formation and retrieval, and influences basic drives such as hunger, thirst, and reproduction.

Cortex: The cortex is the outermost layer of the cerebrum, responsible for higher-order cognitive processes. It consists of gray matter and is densely packed with neurons. The cortex is divided into various areas, each with specialized functions. For example, the frontal cortex is involved in executive functions, such as decision-making and planning, while the occipital cortex processes visual information.

The brain's function relies on the intricate interplay between its various regions and neural networks. Neurons, the building blocks of the brain, transmit electrical and chemical signals to communicate with one another. These signals allow information to flow between different brain regions, enabling us to perceive the world, think, feel emotions, and engage in complex behaviors.

Moreover, the brain is constantly adapting and changing through a process called neuroplasticity. Neural connections can be strengthened, weakened, or formed anew in response to our experiences, thoughts, and behaviors. This plasticity allows the brain to learn, memorize, and rewire itself throughout our lives.

By understanding the brain's structure and function, we gain insight into the intricate mechanisms that underlie our thoughts, emotions, and behaviors. It sets the stage for exploring how gratitude can influence these processes, shape neural pathways, and bring about positive changes in our mental and emotional well-being.

Role of neurotransmitters, such as dopamine and serotonin, in regulating emotions and mood

Neurotransmitters are chemical messengers in the brain that play a vital role in transmitting signals between neurons. These substances are involved in various aspects of brain function, including regulating emotions, mood, and overall mental well-being. Two neurotransmitters that have garnered significant attention in relation to emotions and mood are dopamine and serotonin.

> **Dopamine:** Dopamine is often referred to as the "reward neurotransmitter" due to its role in the brain's reward system. It is involved in experiencing pleasure, motivation, and reinforcement of behaviors. Dopamine also plays a role in regulating movement and cognition.

When we engage in rewarding activities or experience something pleasurable, dopamine is released in specific brain regions, such as the nucleus accumbens and prefrontal cortex. This release of dopamine creates a sense of pleasure and reinforces the behavior, motivating us to seek out similar experiences in the future.

Imbalances in dopamine levels have been associated with various mental health conditions. For example, low levels of dopamine are linked to depression, while high levels may contribute to conditions like schizophrenia. Understanding the role of dopamine helps shed light on how gratitude can influence the brain. Expressing gratitude has been shown to increase dopamine levels, promoting positive emotions and reinforcing the practice of gratitude itself.

> **Serotonin:** Serotonin is another important neurotransmitter that influences mood, emotions, and social behavior. It is involved in regulating sleep, appetite, and pain perception. Serotonin is often associated with feelings of well-being and happiness.

Low levels of serotonin have been implicated in depression and anxiety disorders. Medications targeting serotonin, such as selective serotonin reuptake inhibitors (SSRIs), are commonly used to treat these conditions. These medications work by increasing serotonin levels in the brain, helping to alleviate depressive symptoms.

Gratitude has been found to boost serotonin production and release. When we express gratitude or engage in grateful thinking, it activates brain regions associated with positive emotions and increases serotonin activity. This can contribute to improved mood, reduced anxiety, and overall emotional well-being.

It is important to note that neurotransmitters like dopamine and serotonin do not solely dictate our emotions and mood. The brain's chemical balance is complex, and many factors contribute to our emotional experiences. However, understanding the role of neurotransmitters provides valuable insights into how gratitude can impact our brain chemistry, leading to positive changes in emotions and overall mental health.

By practicing gratitude regularly, we can enhance the activity of these neurotransmitters, fostering positive emotional states, promoting resilience, and contributing to a greater sense of well-being. The influence of gratitude on dopamine and serotonin levels highlights the profound impact that cultivating gratitude can have on our emotional lives.

The concept of neural pathways and their importance in shaping behavior and thought patterns

Within the intricate network of the brain, neural pathways play a crucial role in shaping our behavior and thought patterns. Neural pathways are the connections formed between neurons, allowing information to travel throughout the brain. These pathways are created and strengthened through repeated patterns of thoughts, emotions, and behaviors. Understanding the concept of neural pathways provides insights into how gratitude can influence and reshape our cognitive processes.

> **Formation of Neural Pathways:** Neural pathways are formed through a process called synaptic plasticity. When we engage in specific thoughts, emotions, or behaviors, neurons that fire together strengthen their connections. This phenomenon is often summarized by the phrase, "Neurons that fire together, wire together." Over time, the repeated activation of certain pathways reinforces their strength and efficiency.

For example, imagine learning to ride a bicycle. At first, the neural connections associated with balance and coordination may be weak and uncoordinated. However, with practice, the relevant neural pathways are reinforced, enabling smoother and more effortless cycling. Similarly, our thoughts, emotions, and behaviors can create well-established neural pathways that shape our responses and perceptions.

> **Influence on Behavior and Thought Patterns:** Neural pathways have a profound influence on our behavior and thought patterns. The more frequently we engage in specific thoughts or behaviors, the stronger the corresponding neural pathways become. These pathways form the basis for our habits, automatic responses, and cognitive biases.

For instance, if we often ruminate on negative thoughts or focus on what is lacking in our lives, we strengthen neural pathways associated with negativity and dissatisfaction. Conversely, when we cultivate gratitude and focus on the positive aspects of our experiences, we reinforce pathways linked to optimism and appreciation. By consciously directing our attention and practicing gratitude, we can reshape our neural pathways, leading to more positive thought patterns and behaviors.

> **Plasticity and Change:** The concept of neural plasticity is essential in understanding the potential for change and growth. The brain has the remarkable

ability to reorganize and adapt throughout our lives. This means that even well-established neural pathways can be modified or replaced with new ones.

By incorporating gratitude practices into our daily lives, we can intentionally rewire our neural pathways. As we consistently focus on the things we are grateful for, we strengthen connections associated with positive emotions, well-being, and appreciation. Over time, this can lead to a shift in our default thought patterns, making gratitude a more natural and automatic response.

Understanding the influence of neural pathways highlights the power of gratitude in shaping our thoughts, emotions, and behaviors. By intentionally cultivating gratitude, we can reshape our neural networks, fostering a positive mindset, and promoting a greater sense of well-being. The malleability of neural pathways offers us the opportunity to proactively steer our cognitive processes, leading to a more grateful and fulfilling life.

Chapter 3: Unraveling Neuroplasticity

In this chapter, we will embark on a fascinating exploration of neuroplasticity, the brain's remarkable capacity to change and adapt throughout our lives. Neuroplasticity lies at the heart of understanding how gratitude can transform our neural pathways, reshape our thoughts, and ultimately change our lives. Join us as we delve deeper into the mechanisms and implications of neuroplasticity.

> **What is Neuroplasticity?** Neuroplasticity refers to the brain's ability to reorganize and rewire itself in response to experiences, thoughts, and behaviors. It challenges the long-held notion that the brain's structure and function remain fixed after a certain age. Instead, research has shown that the brain retains its ability to change and adapt, even into adulthood.

Neuroplasticity encompasses several key processes, including synaptic plasticity and neurogenesis. Synaptic plasticity involves the strengthening or weakening of connections between neurons, while neurogenesis refers to the birth of new neurons. These processes underpin our brain's remarkable capacity to learn, remember, and transform throughout our lives.

Mechanisms of Neuroplasticity: Neuroplasticity involves intricate cellular and molecular processes that occur within the brain. When we engage in new experiences, learn new skills, or adopt new thought patterns, neural connections are formed, strengthened, or pruned.

At the cellular level, synaptic plasticity involves changes in the strength and structure of connections between neurons. Long-term potentiation (LTP) and long-term depression (LTD) are two processes that contribute to synaptic plasticity. LTP strengthens synaptic connections, making them more efficient, while LTD weakens or eliminates connections that are no longer needed.

Neurogenesis, on the other hand, occurs primarily in specific regions of the brain, such as the hippocampus. It involves the generation of new neurons from neural stem cells. Neurogenesis plays a critical role in learning, memory, and emotional regulation.

Experience and Neuroplasticity: Our experiences shape the neural pathways in our brains. Positive experiences, including practicing gratitude, engaging in meaningful activities, and learning new skills, have the potential to induce positive changes in the brain. These experiences stimulate the release of neurotransmitters, growth factors, and other molecular signals that promote synaptic plasticity and neurogenesis.

Conversely, negative experiences, chronic stress, and harmful thought patterns can lead to detrimental changes in the brain. They can weaken neural connections, alter neurotransmitter levels, and impair cognitive functioning. However, the brain's plasticity also offers the possibility of reshaping these negative patterns through intentional interventions, such as gratitude practices.

Gratitude and Neuroplasticity: Gratitude has been shown to have a profound impact on neuroplasticity. By consciously cultivating gratitude, we can harness the brain's plasticity to rewire our neural pathways in positive ways. As we consistently focus on the things we are grateful for, we strengthen connections associated with positivity, well-being, and resilience. This can lead to a shift in our default thought patterns, making gratitude a more natural and automatic response.

Research suggests that gratitude practices can increase the thickness of the prefrontal cortex, a region associated with executive functions and emotional regulation. Gratitude also enhances the activity and connectivity within brain networks related to positive emotions and social bonding.

By understanding the mechanisms of neuroplasticity and its interaction with gratitude, we gain insight into the profound potential for personal growth and transformation. As we actively shape our neural pathways through gratitude, we can cultivate a more positive and fulfilling life. Join us as we explore the exciting possibilities that neuroplasticity offers and discover how gratitude can reshape our brains and minds.

Neuroplasticity, also known as brain plasticity, refers to the brain's ability to change and reorganize itself in response to experiences, stimuli, and environmental demands. It is a fundamental property of the brain that allows it to adapt, learn, and recover from injuries or changes in the environment.

The brain is composed of billions of neurons, specialized cells that communicate with each other through electrochemical signals. Neuroplasticity occurs at various levels within the brain, including at the cellular and network levels.

> **Cellular Level:** At the cellular level, neuroplasticity involves changes in the strength and structure of connections between neurons, known as synapses.
>
> These changes can occur through two primary processes:
>
> - **Synaptic Plasticity:** Synaptic plasticity refers to the ability of synapses to change their strength. It involves the strengthening or weakening of connections between neurons. Long-term potentiation (LTP) is a form of synaptic plasticity that strengthens synapses, making them more efficient in transmitting signals. Long-term depression (LTD), on the other hand, weakens or eliminates synapses that

are no longer needed. These processes of synaptic plasticity play a critical role in learning, memory, and information processing.

- **Neurogenesis:** Neurogenesis is the process of generating new neurons in specific regions of the brain, such as the hippocampus. It was once believed that neurogenesis primarily occurred during early development and ceased in adulthood. However, research has shown that new neurons can continue to be generated throughout life, particularly in regions associated with learning and memory. Neurogenesis contributes to the brain's ability to adapt and form new connections in response to experiences and stimuli.

- **Network Level:** Neuroplasticity also occurs at the network level, involving the reorganization and rewiring of neural networks within the brain. This reorganization can happen in response to changes in sensory input, learning new skills, or even as a result of brain injuries. Neural networks that are frequently activated and engaged become strengthened, while those that are underutilized may weaken or undergo pruning.

The brain's ability to change in response to experiences and stimuli is driven by the principle of "neurons that fire together, wire together." When we engage in specific thoughts, behaviors, or experiences, the neural pathways associated with those activities are repeatedly activated. This repetition leads to the strengthening of connections between neurons, making the corresponding neural pathways more efficient.

Conversely, when certain neural pathways are not frequently used or stimulated, they may weaken or even disappear through a process called synaptic pruning. This selective pruning allows the brain to optimize its resources and refine its connectivity.

The concept of neuroplasticity emphasizes that the brain is not a fixed and unchanging organ. Instead, it has the remarkable capacity to adapt, reorganize, and rewire itself throughout life. By understanding neuroplasticity, we can appreciate the brain's ability to learn new skills, recover from injuries, and even transform our thoughts and behaviors. Practicing gratitude, for example, can harness the power of neuroplasticity to shape our brains in positive ways and enhance our overall well-being.

Mechanisms of neuroplasticity, including synaptic pruning, neurogenesis, and myelination

Neuroplasticity, the brain's ability to change and adapt, involves several key mechanisms that contribute to its remarkable flexibility. These mechanisms include synaptic pruning, neurogenesis, and myelination, each playing a vital role in shaping the brain's structure and function in response to experiences.

> **Synaptic Pruning:** Synaptic pruning is a process in which the brain eliminates or reduces the number of synapses, the connections between neurons. During early brain development, the brain produces an abundance of synapses, far more than it needs. As the brain matures and experiences shape its neural circuitry, a process of refinement occurs.

Synaptic pruning involves the selective strengthening of important connections and the elimination of weaker or redundant ones. This pruning process helps to optimize neural networks by preserving the most relevant and frequently used connections while eliminating unnecessary ones. It allows the brain to become more efficient in processing information and improves the overall functionality of neural circuits.

Synaptic pruning primarily occurs during childhood and adolescence but continues throughout adulthood to a lesser extent. It is influenced by environmental factors, experiences, and learning.

> **Neurogenesis:** Neurogenesis refers to the generation of new neurons in the brain. Once thought to be limited to early stages of development, research has shown that neurogenesis can occur in certain brain regions throughout life, particularly in the hippocampus—a region crucial for learning and memory.

Newly generated neurons originate from neural stem cells and undergo a complex process of proliferation, differentiation, and integration into existing neural circuits. Neurogenesis is influenced by various factors, including environmental enrichment, physical exercise, and learning experiences.

The addition of new neurons through neurogenesis can enhance the brain's capacity for learning, memory formation, and cognitive flexibility. It provides an opportunity for the brain to adapt and incorporate new information and experiences.

> **Myelination:** Myelination is the process of forming a protective sheath called myelin around axons, the long, slender projections of neurons. Myelin consists of fatty substances that insulate and increase the speed of electrical impulses traveling along the axon.

During brain development, myelination occurs in a sequential and region-specific manner. It begins in early childhood and continues into adulthood, with different brain regions undergoing myelination at different rates.

Myelination enhances the efficiency and speed of neuronal communication. It helps to coordinate complex neural networks, allowing for rapid and synchronized information processing. The myelin sheath also provides insulation and protection to axons, preserving the integrity of neural connections.

The interplay between synaptic pruning, neurogenesis, and myelination contributes to the brain's ability to adapt and rewire itself. These mechanisms shape the brain's structure and function in response to experiences, learning, and environmental influences. By understanding and harnessing these mechanisms, we can actively promote neuroplasticity and optimize our brain's potential for growth, learning, and positive change.

Examples of neuroplasticity in action and how it relates to gratitude

Neuroplasticity manifests in numerous ways throughout our lives, and understanding its application can shed light on how gratitude can positively impact the brain. Let's explore a few examples of neuroplasticity in action and how they relate to gratitude:

> **Strengthening Neural Pathways:** When we consciously practice gratitude, we are repeatedly activating specific neural pathways associated with positive emotions and appreciation. Through this repetition, the synaptic connections in these pathways become stronger, making gratitude a more natural and automatic response. Over time, our brain becomes wired to notice and focus on the things we are grateful for, fostering a positive outlook.

For instance, as we consistently express gratitude for the kindness of others, our brain strengthens the connections related to empathy and social bonding. This can lead to improved relationships and a heightened sense of connection with others.

> **Rewiring Negative Thought Patterns:** Neuroplasticity enables us to reshape negative thought patterns and cultivate more positive ones. When we engage in gratitude practices, we actively shift our attention towards positive aspects of our lives, redirecting our thoughts away from negativity and rumination.

By consciously focusing on gratitude, we weaken the neural pathways associated with negative thinking and strengthen those related to positivity and well-being. This rewiring allows us to break free from harmful thought patterns and cultivate a more optimistic and grateful mindset.

Changing Brain Structure: Studies have shown that practicing gratitude can have a tangible impact on the structure of the brain. For example, research has suggested that regular gratitude practices can increase the thickness of the prefrontal cortex—a region associated with emotional regulation, decision-making, and perspective-taking.

Additionally, gratitude has been found to enhance the activity and connectivity within brain networks related to positive emotions, social cognition, and reward processing. These changes in brain structure and function contribute to a more resilient and positive mindset.

Alleviating Stress and Improving Mental Health: Chronic stress can have detrimental effects on the brain, leading to anxiety, depression, and cognitive impairments. However, gratitude has been shown to counteract the negative impact of stress by promoting neuroplasticity.

Practicing gratitude can activate the brain's reward circuitry, releasing neurotransmitters like dopamine and serotonin, which contribute to feelings of well-being and happiness. By regularly engaging in gratitude, we can counteract the negative effects of stress on the brain and promote mental health.

These examples highlight how neuroplasticity enables us to actively shape our brain's functioning and structure through gratitude practices. By consciously engaging in gratitude, we harness the brain's capacity to rewire itself, leading to long-lasting positive changes in our thoughts, emotions, and overall well-being. Understanding the interplay between neuroplasticity and gratitude empowers us to cultivate a more grateful mindset and enhance our brain's potential for personal growth and happiness.

Chapter 4: Gratitude and the Brain

In this chapter, we will delve into the fascinating relationship between gratitude and the brain. We will explore how practicing gratitude impacts the brain's structure, function, and overall well-being. Join us as we uncover the remarkable ways in which gratitude shapes our neural pathways and fosters positive change within the brain.

> **Gratitude and Neurochemicals:** When we experience and express gratitude, the brain responds by releasing a cascade of neurochemicals that contribute to our well-being. These neurochemicals, such as dopamine, serotonin, and oxytocin, play crucial roles in regulating mood, emotions, and social bonding.

Dopamine, often referred to as the "feel-good" neurotransmitter, is released when we experience pleasure or reward. Expressing gratitude activates the brain's reward system, leading to an increase in dopamine levels and generating feelings of happiness and contentment.

Serotonin, known for its mood-regulating properties, is also closely linked to gratitude. Gratitude practices have been shown to increase serotonin production in the brain, contributing to a sense of calmness, improved mood, and overall emotional well-being.

Oxytocin, often referred to as the "bonding hormone," is released during social interactions and plays a role in strengthening social connections. Gratitude fosters a sense of connection and appreciation for others, leading to the release of oxytocin and the enhancement of social bonds.

> **Rewiring Neural Pathways:** Practicing gratitude has the power to rewire our neural pathways, shaping our thought patterns and emotions in profound ways. By

consciously focusing on gratitude, we stimulate the brain regions associated with positive emotions, empathy, and social cognition.

Repeatedly activating these neural pathways strengthens the connections and makes gratitude a more automatic response. As a result, we become more attuned to the positive aspects of life, find it easier to navigate challenges, and develop a more optimistic outlook.

Gratitude also promotes neural plasticity, allowing us to break free from negative thought patterns and cultivate resilience. By actively shifting our attention to gratitude, we weaken neural pathways associated with negativity, stress, and anxiety while strengthening those linked to positivity and well-being.

Enhancing Emotional Regulation: Emotional regulation refers to our ability to effectively manage and regulate our emotions. Gratitude plays a crucial role in enhancing emotional regulation by activating the prefrontal cortex, a region responsible for executive functions such as decision-making and emotional control.

Regular gratitude practices increase the thickness of the prefrontal cortex, facilitating better emotional regulation and impulse control. This allows us to respond to challenging situations with greater composure and make more thoughtful decisions.

Promoting Mental Health and Well-being: Gratitude has a significant impact on our overall mental health and well-being. Studies have shown that individuals who regularly practice gratitude experience reduced symptoms of depression, anxiety, and stress.

By rewiring neural pathways, releasing neurochemicals associated with happiness, and enhancing emotional regulation, gratitude acts as a protective factor against mental health challenges. It fosters a positive mindset, cultivates resilience, and promotes a sense of fulfillment and satisfaction.

In this chapter, we have explored how gratitude affects the brain at a neurochemical and neural pathway level. We have seen how expressing gratitude releases neurochemicals that contribute to our happiness and well-being. Additionally, practicing gratitude rewires our neural pathways, enhances emotional regulation, and promotes overall mental health.

Understanding the intricate relationship between gratitude and the brain empowers us to harness the power of gratitude and actively cultivate a grateful mindset. By embracing gratitude, we not only transform our brain but also enrich our lives and create a ripple effect of positivity and well-being.

Scientific studies and research on the neural correlates of gratitude

In recent years, researchers have been investigating the neural correlates of gratitude to understand how it affects the brain and its associated benefits. Through various neuroimaging techniques and studies, significant insights have emerged, shedding light on the underlying neural mechanisms of gratitude. Let's explore some notable scientific findings:

> **Neuroimaging Studies:** Neuroimaging studies, such as functional magnetic resonance imaging (fMRI), have provided valuable insights into the neural correlates of gratitude. These studies have shown that expressing gratitude activates specific brain regions, including:
> - **Prefrontal Cortex (PFC):** The PFC, particularly the medial prefrontal cortex (mPFC), is consistently implicated in gratitude. It plays a vital role in emotion regulation, self-referential processing, and social cognition. Activation of the mPFC during gratitude exercises suggests its involvement in self-reflection and positive appraisal.
> - **Anterior Cingulate Cortex (ACC):** The ACC is involved in emotion processing and conflict resolution. Gratitude practices have been found to activate the ACC,

suggesting its role in regulating emotions and cognitive control during gratitude experiences.

- **Striatum:** The striatum, a region associated with reward processing, is activated when individuals experience and express gratitude. This activation suggests that gratitude may be intrinsically rewarding, leading to positive reinforcement and motivation to engage in further grateful behaviors.

Effects on Neurotransmitters: Gratitude has been linked to changes in neurotransmitter activity, which influences mood and well-being. Research suggests that gratitude practices increase the release of dopamine, serotonin, and other neurotransmitters associated with positive emotions and social bonding.

Increased dopamine levels contribute to feelings of pleasure and reward, while serotonin promotes overall emotional well-being. These neurochemical changes provide a neural basis for the positive emotional effects experienced during gratitude exercises.

Impact on Default Mode Network (DMN): The DMN is a network of brain regions active during rest and self-referential thinking. Gratitude practices have been found to modulate the DMN, leading to reduced activation in regions associated with rumination and self-focus, such as the medial temporal lobe.

By reducing rumination and shifting focus away from negative thoughts, gratitude practices promote a more positive and present-oriented mindset.

Associations with Mental Health: Studies examining the neural correlates of gratitude have also explored its relationship with mental health. Research suggests that individuals who regularly practice gratitude show increased activity in brain regions associated with positive emotions and well-being, while experiencing reduced activity in regions linked to negative emotions and stress.

Gratitude has been found to correlate with lower levels of anxiety, depression, and stress, and improved overall psychological well-being. These findings highlight the potential of gratitude as a protective factor against mental health challenges.

By investigating the neural correlates of gratitude, these studies provide compelling evidence for the beneficial effects of gratitude on the brain. The activation of specific brain regions, modulation of neurotransmitters, and impact on networks associated with emotional regulation contribute to the positive outcomes observed in individuals practicing gratitude.

Understanding the neural correlates of gratitude not only validates its effects but also informs the development of interventions and therapies aimed at enhancing well-being and promoting mental health.

Brain regions associated with gratitude, such as the prefrontal cortex, amygdala, and insula

Gratitude is a complex emotion that involves various brain regions working in harmony. Research has identified several brain regions that play key roles in the experience and expression of gratitude. Let's explore some of the brain regions associated with gratitude:

> **Prefrontal Cortex (PFC):** The prefrontal cortex, particularly the medial prefrontal cortex (mPFC), is consistently implicated in gratitude. The mPFC is involved in self-referential processing, emotional regulation, and social cognition. It plays a vital role in evaluating and appraising positive stimuli, including gratitude-related experiences.

Activation of the mPFC has been observed during gratitude tasks and exercises. This region is involved in self-reflection, processing positive emotions, and attributing value to social interactions and acts of kindness. The mPFC's engagement during gratitude suggests its role in generating positive appraisals and the subjective experience of gratefulness.

> **Amygdala:** The amygdala, a key player in emotion processing, also contributes to the experience of gratitude. The amygdala helps encode and consolidate emotional memories and plays a significant role in social and emotional behaviors.

Studies have shown that the amygdala is activated during gratitude-related experiences. This activation reflects the emotional and social significance of gratitude, particularly in terms of processing the positive valence and social relevance of grateful events or interactions.

Insula: The insula is another brain region associated with gratitude. It is involved in the subjective experience of emotions, interoception (awareness of bodily sensations), and empathy. The insula helps integrate bodily sensations with emotional experiences and plays a role in emotional awareness and empathy towards others.

During gratitude exercises, the insula has shown increased activation. This suggests that gratitude involves an embodied experience, connecting positive emotions and bodily sensations. The insula's involvement in gratitude highlights the interplay between emotions, self-awareness, and social connections.

Ventral Striatum: The ventral striatum, a component of the brain's reward system, is engaged during gratitude experiences. It plays a role in processing reward, motivation, and reinforcement learning. Activation of the ventral striatum during gratitude tasks suggests that gratitude may be intrinsically rewarding and reinforces the motivation to engage in grateful behaviors.

These brain regions work together to create the neural substrates of gratitude. The prefrontal cortex appraises and evaluates gratitude-related stimuli, the amygdala processes the emotional significance, the insula integrates bodily sensations and empathic responses, and the ventral striatum contributes to the rewarding aspects of gratitude.

Understanding the involvement of these brain regions in gratitude provides insights into the neural mechanisms underlying the experience and expression of gratitude. It emphasizes the complexity of gratitude as an emotion that encompasses cognitive, emotional, and social processes. By exploring the activity within these brain regions, we gain a deeper understanding of how gratitude influences our thoughts, emotions, and social connections.

Neurochemical changes observed during gratitude practices and their impact on well-being

Gratitude practices have been shown to induce notable neurochemical changes in the brain, contributing to enhanced well-being and emotional states. Let's explore some of the key neurochemical changes observed during gratitude practices and their impact:

> **Dopamine:** Dopamine, often referred to as the "feel-good" neurotransmitter, plays a crucial role in reward, motivation, and pleasure. Expressing gratitude has been found to increase dopamine levels in the brain.

When we engage in gratitude practices, such as writing a gratitude journal or expressing gratitude to others, dopamine is released, generating feelings of happiness, satisfaction, and contentment. This surge in dopamine reinforces the rewarding nature of gratitude, making it a motivating and enjoyable experience.

The increased dopamine levels not only contribute to immediate positive emotions but also promote long-term well-being by reinforcing the practice of gratitude and encouraging its repetition.

> **Serotonin:** Serotonin is a neurotransmitter associated with mood regulation, emotional well-being, and overall happiness. Gratitude practices have been linked to increased serotonin production in the brain.

By expressing gratitude, we activate neural pathways that stimulate the release of serotonin. This elevation in serotonin levels can contribute to improved mood, reduced anxiety and depression symptoms, and a greater sense of well-being.

Higher serotonin levels are associated with a more positive outlook, increased resilience, and enhanced emotional regulation. Regular gratitude practices can therefore promote a sustained state of emotional well-being and positivity.

> **Oxytocin:** Oxytocin, often referred to as the "bonding hormone," is released during social interactions and plays a role in building trust, empathy, and social connections. Gratitude practices have been found to increase oxytocin levels.

When we express gratitude to others or reflect on acts of kindness, the release of oxytocin fosters a sense of connection, empathy, and appreciation. This neurochemical response enhances social bonding and strengthens relationships.

The increased levels of oxytocin contribute to a greater sense of belonging, improved interpersonal connections, and a deeper appreciation for others. These social benefits further contribute to overall well-being and emotional satisfaction.

The neurochemical changes observed during gratitude practices create a positive feedback loop. The release of dopamine, serotonin, and oxytocin reinforces the experience of gratitude, making it a rewarding and pleasurable activity. As these neurochemical changes become more frequent through consistent gratitude practices, they contribute to long-term improvements in emotional well-being, resilience, and social relationships.

By understanding the neurochemical impact of gratitude, we gain insight into the biological mechanisms that underlie its positive effects. These neurochemical changes provide a scientific basis for the transformative power of gratitude in promoting well-being, happiness, and fulfilling social connections.

Chapter 5: Rewiring the Brain with Gratitude Practices

In this chapter, we will explore how gratitude practices can effectively rewire the brain, creating lasting changes in neural pathways and promoting a more positive and grateful mindset. Discover the transformative potential of gratitude as we delve into various techniques and exercises that facilitate brain rewiring.

> **The Power of Intentional Gratitude:** Intentional gratitude practices involve consciously and deliberately focusing on gratitude in daily life. By directing our attention towards the positive aspects of our experiences, we can reshape the neural pathways associated with negativity and cultivate a more grateful perspective.

We will explore techniques such as keeping a gratitude journal, writing gratitude letters, or engaging in gratitude meditation. These practices encourage us to reflect on the things we appreciate, fostering a mindset that actively seeks out and acknowledges the blessings in our lives.

> **Gratitude and Perspective Shifting:** Gratitude practices help us shift our perspective from scarcity to abundance, from problems to possibilities. By consciously reframing our thoughts and focusing on gratitude, we rewire our neural pathways to recognize and amplify positive experiences.

We will explore techniques like gratitude reframing, where we intentionally reinterpret challenging situations through a lens of gratitude. This exercise helps us find silver linings, learn valuable lessons, and develop resilience in the face of adversity.

Cultivating Mindfulness and Gratitude: Mindfulness practices enhance our ability to be fully present in the moment, fostering a deeper appreciation for the present and the positive aspects of our lives. By combining mindfulness and gratitude, we amplify the rewiring effects on the brain.

We will explore mindfulness techniques such as gratitude meditation, where we cultivate a state of deep awareness and appreciation for the present moment. Through this practice, we strengthen the neural pathways associated with gratitude, presence, and emotional well-being.

Building Gratitude Habits: To rewire the brain effectively, it is important to establish gratitude as a habit. We will discuss strategies for integrating gratitude into our daily routines and making it a natural part of our lives.

We will explore techniques such as gratitude triggers, where we associate specific cues or events with expressions of gratitude. These triggers help us cultivate gratitude as an automatic response, strengthening the neural pathways associated with gratitude and making it a lasting habit.

The Ripple Effect of Gratitude: Gratitude not only rewires our individual brains but also has a positive impact on the people around us. We will explore the ripple effect of gratitude, how expressing gratitude can inspire and influence others, creating a culture of appreciation and kindness.

By spreading gratitude and creating a positive social environment, we contribute to the rewiring of collective neural pathways, fostering well-being and enhancing interpersonal connections.

In this chapter, we have discovered various gratitude practices that effectively rewire the brain. Through intentional gratitude, perspective shifting, mindfulness, habit-building, and the ripple effect, we reshape our neural pathways to embrace a grateful mindset.

By engaging in these gratitude practices consistently, we transform the brain's wiring, making gratitude a natural and automatic response. This rewiring leads to long-lasting changes in emotional well-being, resilience, and interpersonal relationships.

Join us as we embark on the journey of rewiring our brains with gratitude, unlocking the immense power of this transformative practice.

Practical techniques for cultivating gratitude, such as gratitude journaling, meditation, and acts of kindness

Cultivating gratitude is a powerful practice that can positively impact our well-being and transform our mindset. In this section, we will explore practical techniques that you can incorporate into your daily life to cultivate gratitude:

Gratitude Journaling: Keeping a gratitude journal is a popular and effective technique for cultivating gratitude. Set aside a few minutes each day to write down three to five things you are grateful for. They can be simple or significant, ranging from the people in your life to the experiences you've had or the qualities you appreciate in yourself.

By regularly reflecting on the positive aspects of your life and documenting them in a journal, you train your brain to focus on gratitude. This practice rewires your neural pathways to notice and appreciate the abundance in your life.

Gratitude Meditation: Gratitude meditation involves dedicating specific time for focused gratitude practice. Find a quiet and comfortable space, close your eyes, and take a few deep breaths to center yourself. Then, bring to mind the things you are grateful for.

As you focus on each element of gratitude, allow yourself to fully experience the associated emotions. You can visualize the people, experiences, or things you appreciate and mentally express your gratitude towards them.

Gratitude meditation helps strengthen the neural connections associated with gratitude, fostering a sense of contentment and emotional well-being.

Acts of Kindness: Engaging in acts of kindness towards others is a powerful way to cultivate gratitude. Perform simple acts of kindness, such as helping a stranger, expressing appreciation to someone, or volunteering your time for a charitable cause.

Acts of kindness not only create a positive impact on others but also generate feelings of gratitude within yourself. By actively seeking opportunities to be kind, you train your brain to notice the goodness around you and appreciate the interconnectedness of humanity.

Gratitude Walks or Nature Immersion: Spend time in nature and combine it with a gratitude practice. Take a mindful walk in a natural setting, paying attention to the sights, sounds, and sensations around you. As you immerse yourself in nature, reflect on the things you are grateful for in that environment.

Connect with the beauty of nature, the gifts it offers, and the sense of interconnectedness it provides. This practice helps shift your focus to the present moment and cultivates gratitude for the wonders of the natural world.

Gratitude Rituals: Create rituals that incorporate gratitude into your daily routines. For example, you can start or end each day by sharing one thing you are grateful for with a loved one, writing it down, or saying it out loud to yourself.

By integrating gratitude into your rituals, you make it a consistent part of your life, reinforcing the rewiring of your brain towards a grateful mindset.

Remember, consistency is key in cultivating gratitude. Choose the techniques that resonate with you and commit to practicing them regularly. Over time, these practices will become ingrained, and gratitude will become a natural and effortless part of your life.

By incorporating gratitude journaling, meditation, acts of kindness, nature immersion, and gratitude rituals, you actively engage in rewiring your brain towards a more grateful and appreciative outlook. Embrace these practical techniques and experience the transformative power of gratitude in your daily life.

How consistent gratitude practices can reshape neural pathways and strengthen positive emotions

Consistent gratitude practices have the remarkable ability to reshape neural pathways in the brain, leading to a strengthening of positive emotions and a more optimistic outlook. Let's explore how this process unfolds:

Attentional Bias: Our brains have a natural tendency to focus on negative experiences, known as the negativity bias. This bias served an evolutionary purpose by alerting us to potential threats in our environment. However, in today's world, it can lead to a disproportionate focus on the negative aspects of life.

Gratitude practices help counteract this bias by redirecting our attention towards positive experiences. When we regularly engage in gratitude exercises such as journaling, meditation, or acts of kindness, we consciously direct our attention to the things we appreciate and are grateful for. This intentional shift in attention gradually rewires our neural pathways, making us more attuned to the positive aspects of life.

Neural Plasticity: The brain's capacity for neural plasticity allows it to reorganize and create new connections between neurons. By consistently practicing gratitude, we activate specific neural pathways associated with positive emotions and gratitude.

As we engage in gratitude practices over time, the repeated firing of these neural pathways strengthens them. This process, known as Hebbian plasticity, leads to the formation of more robust and efficient neural connections. The more frequently we engage in gratitude practices, the stronger these connections become.

Strengthening Positive Emotions: Gratitude practices not only reshape neural pathways but also strengthen positive emotions. By focusing on and acknowledging the things we are grateful for, we activate the brain's reward system, which includes the release of dopamine and other feel-good neurotransmitters.

As we consistently engage in gratitude practices, the brain becomes more adept at generating and sustaining positive emotions. It becomes easier to access feelings of joy, contentment, and appreciation, leading to an overall increase in well-being.

Cognitive Restructuring: Consistent gratitude practices also contribute to cognitive restructuring, which involves changing the way we think and perceive the world. By actively seeking out and reflecting on positive experiences, we challenge negative thought patterns and cultivate a more positive mindset.

Gratitude helps reframe our interpretations of events, emphasizing the positive aspects and nurturing a more optimistic outlook. This cognitive restructuring further reinforces the rewiring of neural pathways, making positivity and gratitude more automatic and ingrained responses.

By consistently engaging in gratitude practices, we actively reshape our brain's neural pathways, strengthening positive emotions and cultivating a more grateful mindset. Over time, this rewiring leads to a perceptual shift, allowing us to perceive and appreciate the abundance and blessings in our lives more readily.

The transformative power of consistent gratitude practices lies in their ability to rewire our brains, fostering a positive and appreciative outlook. Embrace gratitude as a daily practice, and witness the profound impact it can have on your well-being and perspective on life.

Real-life examples and success stories to inspire readers to incorporate gratitude into their daily lives

Real-life examples and success stories serve as powerful motivators, illustrating how gratitude practices have transformed the lives of individuals. Let's explore a few inspiring stories to encourage readers to incorporate gratitude into their daily lives:

Sarah's Journey to Emotional Well-being: Sarah had been struggling with anxiety and depression for years, feeling trapped in a cycle of negative thoughts. Seeking a way to break free, she started a gratitude journaling practice. Each day, she wrote down three things she was grateful for, no matter how small.

Over time, Sarah noticed a significant shift in her mindset. She became more attuned to the positive aspects of her life, no longer overshadowed by negativity. With consistent gratitude practice, she experienced a reduction in anxiety symptoms and an increase in overall emotional well-being. Gratitude became her anchor, providing a sense of grounding and appreciation for the beauty in everyday life.

Mark's Transformative Relationship Building: Mark had always struggled with forming deep connections and maintaining healthy relationships. Feeling disconnected and lonely, he decided to incorporate gratitude into his interactions with others. He started expressing appreciation and gratitude towards his loved ones for their support, kindness, and presence in his life.

As Mark actively practiced gratitude and acknowledged the positive qualities of those around him, he noticed a profound change in his relationships. His expressions of gratitude strengthened the bonds he shared with others, creating a more positive and nurturing social environment. Mark's journey highlighted how gratitude can be a catalyst for building and sustaining meaningful connections.

> **Emily's Path to Resilience:** Emily faced numerous challenges in her life, including a health issue that caused her physical and emotional distress. In her search for healing, she turned to gratitude meditation. Through regular meditation practices focused on gratitude, she learned to find beauty and gratitude in even the most difficult circumstances.

As Emily deepened her gratitude practice, she cultivated resilience and a new perspective on her challenges. Gratitude became a powerful tool that helped her navigate adversity with grace and strength. Emily's story demonstrates how gratitude can empower individuals to find resilience and transform their relationship with adversity.

These real-life examples illustrate the transformative effects of gratitude practices on individuals' lives. They showcase the power of consistent gratitude in promoting emotional well-being, building strong relationships, and fostering resilience.

As readers immerse themselves in these stories, they are inspired to embark on their own gratitude journey. By incorporating gratitude practices into their daily lives, they can experience similar transformations and embrace the positive impact of gratitude on their well-being and overall outlook.

Remember, each person's gratitude journey is unique. These stories serve as reminders that gratitude has the potential to bring about profound positive change, regardless of the starting point. Embrace the power of gratitude and witness the transformative effects it can have on your own life.

Chapter 6: Integrating Gratitude into Relationships

In this chapter, we will explore the profound impact of gratitude on our relationships with others. Gratitude has the power to strengthen connections, enhance communication, and foster a deeper sense of appreciation and understanding. Let's delve into the ways in which we can integrate gratitude into our relationships.

Expressing Gratitude: Expressing gratitude towards our loved ones is a simple yet powerful way to nurture our relationships. Take the time to acknowledge and appreciate the positive qualities, gestures, and support they bring into your life. Verbalize your gratitude through heartfelt compliments, thank-you notes, or expressions of appreciation.

By openly expressing gratitude, we create a positive and affirming atmosphere in our relationships. This fosters a deeper sense of connection and encourages a reciprocal exchange of gratitude and kindness.

Active Listening: Gratitude involves not only expressing appreciation but also actively listening to others with genuine interest and attention. Practice active listening by fully engaging in conversations, offering your undivided presence, and validating the emotions and experiences of your loved ones.

By demonstrating your willingness to understand and empathize, you create a space where gratitude can flourish. Active listening nurtures deeper connections, strengthens trust, and enhances the quality of your relationships.

Gratitude Rituals Together: Integrating gratitude rituals into your relationships can be a beautiful way to bond and create shared experiences. Establish gratitude practices that you can engage in together, such as gratitude journaling as a couple, sharing daily gratitude reflections, or expressing gratitude before meals or bedtime.

By engaging in gratitude rituals together, you reinforce the importance of gratitude in your relationship. It becomes a shared value, deepening your connection and promoting a culture of appreciation and mutual support.

Random Acts of Kindness: Gratitude extends beyond words; it can also be expressed through actions. Engage in random acts of kindness towards your loved ones, surprising them with thoughtful gestures that show your appreciation and gratitude.

These acts of kindness can be as simple as preparing their favorite meal, offering assistance with a task, or planning a surprise outing. Random acts of kindness nourish relationships, creating a positive and uplifting environment where gratitude thrives.

Forgiveness and Gratitude: Forgiveness plays a crucial role in relationships, allowing for growth, healing, and the renewal of trust. Gratitude can facilitate the process of forgiveness by shifting our focus towards the positive aspects of the relationship and the qualities we appreciate in the other person.

Practice gratitude for the lessons learned, the growth experienced, and the strengths within yourself and your loved ones. By embracing gratitude and forgiveness, you create space for deeper understanding, compassion, and the strengthening of your relationships.

Integrating gratitude into our relationships enhances the quality of connections, fosters appreciation, and promotes a positive and nurturing environment. By expressing gratitude, actively listening, engaging in gratitude rituals together, practicing random acts of kindness, and embracing forgiveness, we create a foundation of gratitude within our relationships.

As you incorporate these practices into your relationships, observe the transformative effects they have on the dynamics and overall well-being of both you and your loved ones. Embrace gratitude as a guiding principle in your relationships, and experience the profound impact it can have on creating lasting connections filled with love, understanding, and appreciation.

Remember, integrating gratitude into relationships is an ongoing process. Nurture and cultivate gratitude within your connections, and watch as it strengthens and deepens the bonds you share with others.

The role of gratitude in fostering healthy relationships and connections

Gratitude plays a pivotal role in fostering healthy relationships and deepening our connections with others. By cultivating a mindset of gratitude, we can enhance communication, promote empathy, and nurture a supportive and loving environment. Let's explore the various ways gratitude contributes to the health of our relationships.

Enhancing Appreciation: Gratitude encourages us to recognize and appreciate the positive aspects of our relationships. When we focus on what we are grateful for in our partners, family members, friends, or colleagues, we cultivate a sense of appreciation for their presence, support, and contributions.

Expressing gratitude allows us to celebrate the qualities, actions, and efforts of others, leading to an increased sense of value and validation within the relationship. This appreciation strengthens the bond and fosters a deepened connection.

Building Trust and Emotional Intimacy: Gratitude creates a nurturing and safe space where trust can flourish. When we express gratitude for the trust we have in our loved ones or acknowledge their trustworthiness, it deepens the emotional intimacy and strengthens the foundation of the relationship.

By recognizing and appreciating the trust present in our relationships, we foster an environment of openness, vulnerability, and authenticity. This, in turn, promotes deeper connections and allows for the growth and development of meaningful relationships.

Promoting Empathy and Understanding: Gratitude encourages us to see beyond our own needs and perspectives, enabling us to empathize with others and understand their experiences. By expressing gratitude for the qualities and actions of our loved ones, we develop a greater understanding of their unique perspectives, challenges, and strengths.

Gratitude fosters empathy and compassion, as it reminds us of the impact others have on our lives and the goodness they bring. This understanding nurtures a supportive and empathetic approach to our relationships, creating a space where individuals feel heard, valued, and understood.

Resolving Conflict and Nurturing Forgiveness: Gratitude plays a crucial role in conflict resolution and forgiveness within relationships. When we focus on what we appreciate about the other person, it shifts our attention from grievances to the positive aspects of the relationship.

Expressing gratitude during challenging times can help diffuse tension and promote a more constructive approach to resolving conflicts. Gratitude reminds us of the strengths, shared experiences, and love within the relationship, facilitating forgiveness and fostering a sense of reconciliation.

Cultivating Positivity and Resilience: Gratitude nurtures a positive mindset and resilience within relationships. When we regularly practice gratitude, we train our minds to seek and focus on the positive aspects of our relationships, even during difficult times.

By acknowledging and expressing gratitude for the support, love, and joy present in our connections, we create a foundation of positivity that sustains us during challenging periods. This positivity enhances our resilience, allowing us to navigate obstacles with grace and strength.

Incorporating gratitude into our relationships promotes appreciation, trust, empathy, forgiveness, and positivity. By actively cultivating gratitude within our connections, we create an environment that nurtures and sustains healthy, fulfilling, and loving relationships.

Embrace gratitude as a guiding principle in your interactions, express appreciation regularly, and encourage open and honest communication. As you do so, you will witness the transformative power of gratitude in fostering healthy relationships and deepening your connections with others.

Tips on expressing gratitude to loved ones and creating a gratitude culture within families, friendships, and workplaces

Expressing gratitude is a powerful way to strengthen relationships and foster a culture of appreciation. Whether it's within your family, friendships, or workplace, creating a gratitude culture can have a profound impact on the overall well-being and dynamics of the group. Here are some tips on expressing gratitude and cultivating a gratitude culture:

Be Specific and Sincere: When expressing gratitude, be specific about what you appreciate. Instead of a generic "thank you," highlight the specific actions, qualities, or support that you are grateful for. This shows sincerity and makes the expression of gratitude more meaningful and personal.

For example, instead of saying, "Thanks for everything you do," you could say, "I really appreciate how you always lend a helping hand when I need it. It means a lot to me."

Make it a Habit: Incorporate regular gratitude practices into your routine. This could be as simple as starting or ending each day by expressing one thing you are grateful for within your family, friendship circle, or workplace. Encourage others to participate and create a shared gratitude ritual that everyone can look forward to.

Write Thank-You Notes: Take the time to write heartfelt thank-you notes or messages to express your gratitude. Handwritten notes can be particularly impactful, as they demonstrate effort and thoughtfulness. Be specific in your note, mentioning the person's actions, words, or qualities that you appreciate.

Show Appreciation Through Actions: Gratitude can be expressed not only through words but also through actions. Consider performing random acts of kindness for your loved ones or colleagues to show your appreciation. It could be bringing them their favorite snack, offering to help with a task, or surprising them with a small gift. These acts of kindness speak volumes and convey your gratitude in a tangible way.

Celebrate Achievements and Milestones: Take the time to celebrate the achievements and milestones of your loved ones, friends, or coworkers. Acknowledge their hard work, dedication, or personal accomplishments. Organize a small gathering, send a congratulatory message, or give a thoughtful gift to commemorate their success. This demonstrates that their efforts and achievements are valued and celebrated.

Foster a Supportive Environment: Encourage a culture of gratitude and support within your family, friendship circle, or workplace. Create opportunities for open and honest communication, where expressing appreciation and gratitude is encouraged and valued. Celebrate each other's successes, provide words of encouragement during challenging times, and offer support and empathy when needed.

Lead by Example: Be a role model for gratitude by consistently expressing appreciation and gratitude towards others. Your actions and words have a ripple effect, inspiring those around you to adopt a similar mindset. When others witness your genuine gratitude, they are more likely to follow suit and contribute to a culture of appreciation.

Remember, creating a gratitude culture takes time and consistent effort. Be patient and persistent in your gratitude practices, and encourage others to join in. As gratitude becomes an integral part of your family, friendship, or workplace dynamics, you will witness the positive impact it has on relationships, overall well-being, and the sense of connection within the group.

By expressing gratitude, showing appreciation through actions, and fostering a supportive environment, you can create a culture where gratitude thrives, bringing joy, positivity, and a deeper sense of connection to your relationships and social circles.

The reciprocal nature of gratitude and its potential to enhance social bonds

Gratitude has a reciprocal nature, meaning that expressing gratitude not only benefits the recipient but also strengthens the social bonds between individuals. When gratitude is expressed and received, it creates a positive feedback loop that nurtures and deepens relationships. Let's delve into the reciprocal nature of gratitude and its potential to enhance social bonds.

> **Strengthening Emotional Connection:** When we express gratitude towards someone, it communicates our appreciation and acknowledges their positive impact in our lives. This act of gratitude not only uplifts the recipient but also strengthens the emotional connection between individuals. The recipient feels valued, validated, and understood, fostering a deeper sense of connection and trust.

In turn, when we receive gratitude from others, we experience a sense of validation and recognition for our efforts, which boosts our self-esteem and deepens our emotional connection with the person expressing gratitude. This reciprocity creates a positive and supportive environment that strengthens social bonds.

Cultivating a Culture of Appreciation: When gratitude is consistently expressed within a social group, it cultivates a culture of appreciation. As individuals witness and experience the positive impact of gratitude, they are more likely to adopt a similar mindset and express gratitude towards others.

In a culture of appreciation, social bonds are enhanced as people feel valued, respected, and acknowledged. This creates a positive and nurturing environment where individuals are more likely to support, encourage, and uplift each other.

Encouraging Prosocial Behavior: Gratitude has the power to inspire prosocial behavior, such as acts of kindness, generosity, and support. When we receive gratitude from others, it generates a sense of gratitude within us, motivating us to reciprocate and contribute to the well-being of those around us.

As individuals engage in prosocial behavior, it strengthens social bonds by fostering a sense of reciprocity and mutual support. The act of giving and receiving gratitude creates a positive cycle of kindness and empathy, deepening the connections between individuals.

Promoting Positive Communication: Gratitude facilitates positive communication and healthy interactions within social relationships. When gratitude is expressed, it opens up channels of communication and encourages individuals to share their feelings, thoughts, and appreciation openly.

By fostering positive communication, gratitude allows for deeper understanding, empathy, and connection. It creates a safe space where individuals feel comfortable expressing themselves and strengthening their social bonds through meaningful conversations.

Building Trust and Support: Gratitude plays a vital role in building trust and support within social bonds. When we express gratitude, it demonstrates our recognition of others' contributions, efforts, and qualities. This acknowledgment fosters trust as it signifies our appreciation for their presence and support.

As trust grows, social bonds strengthen, creating a foundation of support and reliability. The reciprocity of gratitude deepens the sense of trust, reinforcing the bonds between individuals.

By understanding the reciprocal nature of gratitude, we can harness its power to enhance social bonds. Expressing gratitude fosters emotional connection, cultivates a culture of appreciation, encourages prosocial behavior, promotes positive communication, and builds trust and support. Embrace the power of gratitude within your relationships, and witness how its reciprocal nature strengthens and enriches the social bonds you share with others.

Chapter 7: Gratitude as a Tool for Resilience and Mental Health

Introduction: In this chapter, we explore the profound impact of gratitude on resilience and mental health. Gratitude serves as a powerful tool that can transform our mindset, enhance our well-being, and bolster our ability to navigate life's challenges. Let us delve into the ways in which gratitude cultivates resilience and promotes positive mental health.

Cultivating Resilience through Gratitude: Resilience refers to our ability to adapt and bounce back from adversity. Gratitude plays a significant role in building resilience by shifting our focus from negative experiences to positive aspects of our lives. Here are some ways gratitude can enhance resilience:

- **Perspective Shift:** Gratitude helps us reframe challenging situations by focusing on the lessons learned, personal growth, and silver linings. It encourages us to see difficulties as opportunities for resilience and development.

- **Positive Coping:** Expressing gratitude during tough times can act as a coping mechanism, providing emotional support and strength. Gratitude reminds us of the resources, support systems, and inner strengths we possess, helping us navigate adversity with a more optimistic mindset.

- **Increased Self-Efficacy:** Gratitude fosters a sense of empowerment and self-belief. When we acknowledge and appreciate our own strengths, as well as the support we receive from others, it enhances our self-efficacy—the belief in our ability to overcome challenges.

Gratitude's Impact on Mental Health: Gratitude has profound effects on mental health, contributing to overall well-being and happiness. Here's how gratitude influences our mental health:

- **Positive Emotion Regulation:** Gratitude helps regulate emotions by shifting our focus towards positive experiences. It reduces the impact of negative emotions, such as stress, anxiety, and depression, by promoting a more positive outlook.

- **Stress Reduction:** Gratitude acts as a buffer against stress, helping to reduce its impact on our mental health. When we cultivate gratitude, we become more resilient to stressors and better equipped to cope with them.

- **Enhanced Psychological Well-being:** Regular gratitude practices have been linked to increased life satisfaction, happiness, and positive mood. Gratitude fosters a sense of contentment, appreciation for the present moment, and a focus on what truly matters.

- **Improved Relationships:** Gratitude strengthens social connections, and positive relationships have a significant impact on mental health. When we express gratitude towards others, it deepens our bonds, provides a sense of belonging, and fosters social support, all of which contribute to better mental well-being.

Gratitude as a Therapeutic Tool: Gratitude has been incorporated into various therapeutic approaches due to its positive impact on mental health. Therapists often use gratitude exercises to help individuals reframe negative thoughts, enhance resilience, and cultivate a more positive mindset.

- **Gratitude Journaling:** Keeping a gratitude journal, where one writes down things they are grateful for, is a common gratitude exercise. It encourages reflection, shifts focus towards positive experiences, and promotes a sense of gratitude on a daily basis.

- **Gratitude Meditation:** Mindfulness-based gratitude meditation involves focusing on feelings of gratitude, acknowledging them, and sending gratitude to oneself and others. It cultivates a deep sense of appreciation and helps train the mind to notice and savor positive experiences.

- **Gratitude in Therapy:** Therapists may incorporate gratitude interventions as part of their treatment plans. This may involve discussing and exploring the role of gratitude in one's life, identifying areas for gratitude, and integrating gratitude practices into daily routines.

Conclusion: Gratitude serves as a transformative tool for resilience and mental health. By cultivating gratitude, we shift our perspective, build resilience, and promote positive mental well-being. Incorporating gratitude practices, such as journaling, meditation, and therapeutic interventions, can significantly enhance our ability to navigate challenges and lead fulfilling lives. Embrace the power of gratitude as a pathway to resilience and improved mental health.

How gratitude practices can boost resilience and help manage stress, anxiety, and depression

Gratitude practices have a profound impact on resilience and can be effective tools for managing stress, anxiety, and depression. By incorporating gratitude into our daily lives, we can cultivate a positive mindset, enhance emotional well-being, and build resilience. Let's explore how gratitude practices can boost resilience and help manage these common mental health challenges:

Shifting Focus and Perspective: Gratitude practices encourage us to shift our focus from negative thoughts and experiences to positive aspects of our lives. By intentionally directing our attention towards what we are grateful for, we reframe our perspective and create a more optimistic outlook. This shift in focus helps us develop resilience by acknowledging the positive aspects amidst challenges and cultivating a sense of hope.

Increasing Positive Emotion: Expressing gratitude stimulates the production of positive emotions, such as joy, contentment, and happiness. These positive emotions act as a counterbalance to stress, anxiety, and depression. By regularly engaging in gratitude practices, we train our minds to actively seek out and appreciate positive experiences, which can help alleviate the symptoms of these mental health conditions.

Cultivating Mindfulness and Presence: Gratitude practices often involve being mindful and present in the moment. By consciously acknowledging and appreciating the present moment, we cultivate a greater sense of awareness and connection to our surroundings. This mindfulness reduces rumination, worry, and negative thoughts associated with stress, anxiety, and depression. It helps us stay grounded and better equipped to manage challenging situations.

Promoting Self-Compassion: Gratitude practices encourage self-compassion, which is vital for managing stress, anxiety, and depression. When we express gratitude towards ourselves, we acknowledge our own strengths, achievements, and resilience. This self-appreciation fosters a sense of self-worth and nurtures a compassionate attitude towards ourselves, counteracting negative self-talk and promoting mental well-being.

Building Social Support: Gratitude practices often involve expressing gratitude towards others. By doing so, we strengthen our social connections and build a support network. Social support is essential for managing stress, anxiety, and depression, as it provides a sense of belonging, validation, and understanding.

Gratitude practices enhance these social bonds, offering a source of comfort and encouragement during difficult times.

Enhancing Resilience: Regular gratitude practices contribute to the development of resilience. By focusing on what we are grateful for, even in challenging circumstances, we reinforce our ability to bounce back from adversity. Gratitude helps us recognize our inner strengths, resources, and support systems, empowering us to navigate stressful situations with resilience and optimism.

Creating Positive Habits: Consistency is key when it comes to gratitude practices. By making gratitude a regular habit, we train our brains to actively seek out positive experiences and appreciate them. Over time, this rewires our neural pathways, making positive thinking and gratitude more automatic. This rewiring process strengthens resilience, making us more adept at managing stress, anxiety, and depression.

Incorporating gratitude practices, such as keeping a gratitude journal, engaging in gratitude meditation, or regularly expressing gratitude to others, can be transformative in managing stress, anxiety, and depression. By harnessing the power of gratitude, we can boost resilience, cultivate positive emotions, and develop effective coping strategies to navigate life's challenges with greater ease and well-being.

The link between gratitude and self-esteem, self-worth, and overall mental well-being

Gratitude is intimately connected to self-esteem, self-worth, and overall mental well-being. When we cultivate gratitude, it has a profound impact on how we perceive ourselves, our worth, and our overall mental state. Let's explore the link between gratitude and these essential aspects of our well-being:

Enhanced Self-Esteem: Gratitude plays a crucial role in boosting self-esteem. When we practice gratitude, we shift our focus from what is lacking to what we have and appreciate about ourselves. This shift in perspective allows us to recognize our strengths, accomplishments, and positive qualities. By acknowledging and valuing our own worth, gratitude fosters a sense of self-esteem and confidence.

Increased Self-Worth: Gratitude reinforces our sense of self-worth. When we express gratitude for the people, experiences, and opportunities in our lives, we affirm our inherent value and deservingness of such blessings. Gratitude helps us recognize that we are worthy of love, happiness, and success, enhancing our self-worth and promoting a healthier self-image.

Positive Self-Perception: Practicing gratitude nurtures a positive self-perception. By focusing on what we are grateful for, we train our minds to seek out the positive aspects of ourselves and our lives. This positive self-perception contributes to greater mental well-being and a more optimistic outlook. Gratitude allows us to see ourselves in a more compassionate and accepting light, fostering a healthier relationship with ourselves.

Reduced Negative Self-Talk: Gratitude acts as a counterbalance to negative self-talk. When we engage in gratitude practices, we intentionally shift our attention away from self-criticism and self-judgment. Instead, we cultivate a mindset of self-acceptance and appreciation. This shift in thinking reduces the frequency and intensity of negative self-talk, promoting a more positive and supportive internal dialogue.

Improved Mental Well-being: Gratitude is strongly associated with improved mental well-being. Regularly practicing gratitude has been linked to increased levels of happiness, life satisfaction, and positive mood. By focusing on what we are grateful for, we train our minds to notice and savor positive experiences. This positive focus enhances our overall mental state, reducing symptoms of anxiety, depression, and stress.

Resilience and Coping: Gratitude plays a role in building resilience and effective coping mechanisms. When we practice gratitude, we acknowledge and appreciate the resources, support systems, and inner strengths we possess. This recognition fosters resilience, as we become better equipped to face challenges and navigate adversity. Gratitude acts as a buffer against negative emotions, reinforcing our mental well-being and ability to cope with life's ups and downs.

Cultivation of Positive Mindset: Gratitude cultivates a positive mindset, which is fundamental to overall mental well-being. By regularly focusing on what we are grateful for, we rewire our brains to notice and appreciate the positive aspects of life. This positive mindset allows us to approach challenges with optimism, find meaning in difficult situations, and maintain a sense of hope and resilience.

Incorporating gratitude practices into our lives can have a transformative effect on self-esteem, self-worth, and overall mental well-being. By nurturing a positive self-perception, reducing negative self-talk, and cultivating resilience, gratitude empowers us to lead happier, more fulfilling lives. Embrace the power of gratitude as a pathway to greater self-esteem, self-worth, and mental well-being.

Evidence-based strategies for incorporating gratitude into therapy and personal growth

Incorporating gratitude into therapy and personal growth can have profound benefits for mental health and overall well-being. Numerous studies have demonstrated the effectiveness of gratitude-based interventions in promoting positive outcomes. Here are evidence-based strategies for incorporating gratitude into therapy and personal growth:

Gratitude Journaling: Gratitude journaling involves regularly writing down things we are grateful for. It is a simple yet powerful practice that can be integrated into therapy and personal growth. Clients can be encouraged to keep a gratitude journal, noting three things they are grateful for each day. This practice helps shift focus towards positive experiences and cultivates a mindset of gratitude.

Three Good Things Exercise: The Three Good Things exercise involves identifying and reflecting on three positive experiences from the day. Clients can be guided to recall specific moments, events, or interactions that brought them joy, gratitude, or a sense of accomplishment. This exercise enhances positive emotions, promotes gratitude, and strengthens resilience.

Gratitude Letter Writing: Gratitude letter writing involves expressing gratitude to someone who has had a positive impact on our lives. In therapy, clients can be encouraged to write gratitude letters to significant individuals, expressing appreciation and acknowledging the influence they have had. This practice enhances positive emotions, strengthens social connections, and fosters a sense of gratitude.

Gratitude Meditation: Mindfulness-based gratitude meditation involves focusing on feelings of gratitude, cultivating a deep sense of appreciation, and directing gratitude towards oneself and others. Therapists can guide clients through gratitude meditation exercises, helping them develop a greater awareness of gratitude and its positive effects on well-being.

Acts of Kindness: Engaging in acts of kindness is another way to incorporate gratitude into therapy and personal growth. Encouraging clients to perform small acts of kindness for others, such as offering assistance or expressing appreciation, can boost feelings of gratitude and promote a sense of purpose and connection.

Gratitude Rituals: Integrating gratitude rituals into daily routines can be beneficial. Therapists can guide clients to establish specific gratitude rituals, such as starting or ending the day with a gratitude reflection or incorporating gratitude into daily affirmations. These rituals reinforce the practice of gratitude and create a sense of consistency and structure.

Group Gratitude Exercises: In group therapy settings, incorporating gratitude exercises can foster a supportive and positive environment. Group members can take turns sharing what they are grateful for, offering encouragement, and expressing appreciation for one another. This practice promotes a sense of community, support, and shared gratitude.

Integration with Cognitive-Behavioral Therapy (CBT): Gratitude can be integrated into Cognitive-Behavioral Therapy (CBT) interventions. Therapists can help clients identify and challenge negative thought patterns, replacing them with gratitude-based reframes. This integration enhances positive thinking, promotes resilience, and fosters a more optimistic outlook.

It is important to tailor gratitude interventions to individual client needs, preferences, and therapeutic goals. Therapists should assess and monitor the impact of gratitude practices on clients' well-being and adjust interventions accordingly. By incorporating evidence-based gratitude strategies, therapy and personal growth journeys can be enriched, leading to improved mental health and overall flourishing.

Conclusion

In conclusion, this book has explored the powerful effects of gratitude on the brain and its transformative potential in our lives. We have delved into the understanding of gratitude, its evolutionary origins, and its significance in human psychology. We have explored the brain's structure and function, as well as the role of neurotransmitters and neural pathways in shaping our thoughts and behavior. Furthermore, we have examined the concept of neuroplasticity and how the brain changes in response to experiences and stimuli.

Throughout the book, we have discovered the profound link between gratitude and the brain. We have explored scientific studies and research that highlight the neural correlates of gratitude, including the involvement of brain regions such as the prefrontal cortex, amygdala, and insula. We have also discussed the neurochemical changes observed during gratitude practices and their impact on our well-being.

The book has provided practical techniques for cultivating gratitude, such as gratitude journaling, meditation, and acts of kindness. We have seen how consistent gratitude practices can reshape neural pathways and strengthen positive emotions. Real-life examples and success stories have inspired us to incorporate gratitude into our daily lives.

Moreover, we have explored how gratitude extends beyond the individual and can be integrated into relationships, fostering healthy connections and enhancing social bonds. We have discussed the reciprocal nature of gratitude, emphasizing its potential to create a culture of appreciation within families, friendships, and workplaces.

Additionally, the book has shed light on the profound impact of gratitude on resilience and mental health. We have discovered how gratitude practices can boost resilience, manage stress, anxiety, and depression. By cultivating gratitude, we can enhance self-esteem, self-worth, and overall mental well-being. Gratitude has the power to reframe our perspective, reduce negative self-talk, and promote a positive mindset.

Lastly, the book has provided evidence-based strategies for incorporating gratitude into therapy and personal growth. These strategies have demonstrated their effectiveness in enhancing positive outcomes and promoting well-being.

In essence, gratitude has the transformative power to change our brains and, ultimately, our lives. By embracing gratitude and incorporating it into our daily practices, we can experience improved well-being, enhanced relationships, increased resilience, and a greater sense of fulfillment. Let us embark on this journey of gratitude, rewiring our brains for a more joyful, meaningful, and fulfilling existence.

As you reach the end of this book, I want to leave you with a heartfelt encouragement to embark on a gratitude journey. The insights and knowledge you have gained about the transformative power of gratitude on the brain have opened a doorway to a more fulfilling and joyful life.

Gratitude is not merely an abstract concept or a passing trend; it is a practice, a way of life that holds the potential to profoundly shape your well-being and the quality of your relationships. It is a tool that empowers you to rewire your brain, to cultivate positivity, and to find solace and strength even in the face of challenges.

I urge you to take the first step on this journey by incorporating gratitude into your daily life. Begin with simple practices such as gratitude journaling, where you can capture and reflect upon the blessings, big and small, that fill your days. Explore the power of gratitude meditation, allowing yourself to immerse in the present moment and embrace a deep sense of appreciation for all that surrounds you.

Extend gratitude beyond yourself and express it to your loved ones, colleagues, and even strangers. Let gratitude become a language of kindness and appreciation that fosters deeper connections and strengthens the bonds that enrich your life.

Embrace the mindset of gratitude and let it permeate your thoughts, actions, and interactions. Notice the beauty in the world around you, savor the little joys, and find gratitude even in the midst of adversity. Allow gratitude to become a habit, a way of seeing and experiencing the world that fills your heart with warmth and positivity.

Remember, the benefits of gratitude are not fleeting or superficial. By embarking on this gratitude journey, you are giving yourself the gift of improved mental health, increased resilience, enhanced self-esteem, and more fulfilling relationships. You are rewiring your brain for happiness, compassion, and a profound sense of well-being.

So, I invite you to take this leap, to embrace the transformative power of gratitude and weave it into the fabric of your life. Let gratitude be the guiding light that illuminates your path and infuses your days with joy and contentment. You have the power to shape your brain, your experiences, and your destiny through the practice of gratitude.

May your gratitude journey be filled with countless moments of appreciation, profound connections, and the discovery of inner strength. Embrace gratitude, and let it unlock the endless possibilities that lie within you. Your brain awaits the transformation, and a more fulfilling life beckons you.

Embrace gratitude. Begin your journey today.

JOURNAL ENTRY DATE:

WHAT ARE YOUR VALUES?

WHAT ARE YOUR PRIORITIES?

WHAT ARE YOUR BOUNDARIES?

WHAT ARE YOUR TOP 3 GOALS?

JOURNAL ENTRY DATE:

WHAT ARE YOUR VALUES?

WHAT ARE YOUR PRIORITIES?

WHAT ARE YOUR BOUNDARIES?

WHAT ARE YOUR TOP 3 GOALS?

JOURNAL ENTRY DATE:

WHAT ARE YOUR VALUES?

WHAT ARE YOUR PRIORITIES?

WHAT ARE YOUR BOUNDARIES?

WHAT ARE YOUR TOP 3 GOALS?

JOURNAL ENTRY DATE:

WHAT ARE YOUR VALUES?

WHAT ARE YOUR PRIORITIES?

WHAT ARE YOUR BOUNDARIES?

WHAT ARE YOUR TOP 3 GOALS?

JOURNAL ENTRY DATE:

WHAT ARE YOUR VALUES?

WHAT ARE YOUR PRIORITIES?

WHAT ARE YOUR BOUNDARIES?

WHAT ARE YOUR TOP 3 GOALS?

JOURNAL ENTRY DATE:

WHAT ARE YOUR VALUES?

WHAT ARE YOUR PRIORITIES?

WHAT ARE YOUR BOUNDARIES?

WHAT ARE YOUR TOP 3 GOALS?

JOURNAL ENTRY DATE:

WHAT ARE YOUR VALUES?

WHAT ARE YOUR PRIORITIES?

WHAT ARE YOUR BOUNDARIES?

WHAT ARE YOUR TOP 3 GOALS?

JOURNAL ENTRY DATE:

WHAT ARE YOUR VALUES?

WHAT ARE YOUR PRIORITIES?

WHAT ARE YOUR BOUNDARIES?

WHAT ARE YOUR TOP 3 GOALS?

JOURNAL ENTRY DATE:

WHAT ARE YOUR VALUES?

WHAT ARE YOUR PRIORITIES?

WHAT ARE YOUR BOUNDARIES?

WHAT ARE YOUR TOP 3 GOALS?

JOURNAL ENTRY DATE:

WHAT ARE YOUR VALUES?

WHAT ARE YOUR PRIORITIES?

WHAT ARE YOUR BOUNDARIES?

WHAT ARE YOUR TOP 3 GOALS?

JOURNAL ENTRY DATE:

WHAT ARE YOUR VALUES?

WHAT ARE YOUR PRIORITIES?

WHAT ARE YOUR BOUNDARIES?

WHAT ARE YOUR TOP 3 GOALS?

JOURNAL ENTRY DATE:

WHAT ARE YOUR VALUES?

WHAT ARE YOUR PRIORITIES?

WHAT ARE YOUR BOUNDARIES?

WHAT ARE YOUR TOP 3 GOALS?

JOURNAL ENTRY DATE:

WHAT ARE YOUR VALUES?

WHAT ARE YOUR PRIORITIES?

WHAT ARE YOUR BOUNDARIES?

WHAT ARE YOUR TOP 3 GOALS?

JOURNAL ENTRY DATE:

WHAT ARE YOUR VALUES?

WHAT ARE YOUR PRIORITIES?

WHAT ARE YOUR BOUNDARIES?

WHAT ARE YOUR TOP 3 GOALS?

JOURNAL ENTRY DATE:

WHAT ARE YOUR VALUES?

WHAT ARE YOUR PRIORITIES?

WHAT ARE YOUR BOUNDARIES?

WHAT ARE YOUR TOP 3 GOALS?

JOURNAL ENTRY DATE:

WHAT ARE YOUR VALUES?

WHAT ARE YOUR PRIORITIES?

WHAT ARE YOUR BOUNDARIES?

WHAT ARE YOUR TOP 3 GOALS?

JOURNAL ENTRY DATE:

WHAT ARE YOUR VALUES?

WHAT ARE YOUR PRIORITIES?

WHAT ARE YOUR BOUNDARIES?

WHAT ARE YOUR TOP 3 GOALS?

JOURNAL ENTRY DATE:

WHAT ARE YOUR VALUES?

WHAT ARE YOUR PRIORITIES?

WHAT ARE YOUR BOUNDARIES?

WHAT ARE YOUR TOP 3 GOALS?

JOURNAL ENTRY DATE:

WHAT ARE YOUR VALUES?

WHAT ARE YOUR PRIORITIES?

WHAT ARE YOUR BOUNDARIES?

WHAT ARE YOUR TOP 3 GOALS?

JOURNAL ENTRY DATE:

WHAT ARE YOUR VALUES?

WHAT ARE YOUR PRIORITIES?

WHAT ARE YOUR BOUNDARIES?

WHAT ARE YOUR TOP 3 GOALS?

JOURNAL ENTRY DATE:

WHAT ARE YOUR VALUES?

WHAT ARE YOUR PRIORITIES?

WHAT ARE YOUR BOUNDARIES?

WHAT ARE YOUR TOP 3 GOALS?

JOURNAL ENTRY DATE:

WHAT ARE YOUR VALUES?

WHAT ARE YOUR PRIORITIES?

WHAT ARE YOUR BOUNDARIES?

WHAT ARE YOUR TOP 3 GOALS?

JOURNAL ENTRY DATE:

WHAT ARE YOUR VALUES?

WHAT ARE YOUR PRIORITIES?

WHAT ARE YOUR BOUNDARIES?

WHAT ARE YOUR TOP 3 GOALS?

JOURNAL ENTRY DATE:

WHAT ARE YOUR VALUES?

WHAT ARE YOUR PRIORITIES?

WHAT ARE YOUR BOUNDARIES?

WHAT ARE YOUR TOP 3 GOALS?

JOURNAL ENTRY DATE:

WHAT ARE YOUR VALUES?

WHAT ARE YOUR PRIORITIES?

WHAT ARE YOUR BOUNDARIES?

WHAT ARE YOUR TOP 3 GOALS?

JOURNAL ENTRY DATE:

WHAT ARE YOUR VALUES?

WHAT ARE YOUR PRIORITIES?

WHAT ARE YOUR BOUNDARIES?

WHAT ARE YOUR TOP 3 GOALS?

JOURNAL ENTRY DATE:

WHAT ARE YOUR VALUES?

WHAT ARE YOUR PRIORITIES?

WHAT ARE YOUR BOUNDARIES?

WHAT ARE YOUR TOP 3 GOALS?

JOURNAL ENTRY DATE:

WHAT ARE YOUR VALUES?

WHAT ARE YOUR PRIORITIES?

WHAT ARE YOUR BOUNDARIES?

WHAT ARE YOUR TOP 3 GOALS?

JOURNAL ENTRY DATE:

WHAT ARE YOUR VALUES?

WHAT ARE YOUR PRIORITIES?

WHAT ARE YOUR BOUNDARIES?

WHAT ARE YOUR TOP 3 GOALS?

JOURNAL ENTRY DATE:

WHAT ARE YOUR VALUES?

WHAT ARE YOUR PRIORITIES?

WHAT ARE YOUR BOUNDARIES?

WHAT ARE YOUR TOP 3 GOALS?

JOURNAL ENTRY DATE:

WHAT ARE YOUR VALUES?

WHAT ARE YOUR PRIORITIES?

WHAT ARE YOUR BOUNDARIES?

WHAT ARE YOUR TOP 3 GOALS?

JOURNAL ENTRY DATE:

WHAT ARE YOUR VALUES?

WHAT ARE YOUR PRIORITIES?

WHAT ARE YOUR BOUNDARIES?

WHAT ARE YOUR TOP 3 GOALS?

Printed in Great Britain
by Amazon